music minus one bass-baritone

4056

BASS-BARITONE ARIAS *with Orchestra*

MOZART: Le Nozze Di Figaro -Conte- *"Vedrò mentr'io sospiro"*
MOZART: Le Nozze Di Figaro -Figaro- *"Se vuol ballare"*
ROSSINI: The Barber of Seville -Basilio- *Aria*
VERDI: Simon Boccanegra -Fiesco- *Aria*
PUCCINI: La Boheme -Colline- *Aria*

A Note on the Arias

Mozart's famous and magnificent *Le Nozze di Figaro* is an opera that almost never was. Beaumarchais' play, which formed its basis, had been banned by Emperor Joseph II, and it was only due to the craftiness of librettist Da Ponte, who was able to convince Joseph to go against his own decree and allow the production, that we owe its existence. And it remains as charming and hilarious as it was at its Vienna premiere in 1786.

Its complicated plot primarily involves two couples: the Count and Countess Almaviva; and the Countess's maid, Susanna, and her betrothed, the Count's valet, Figaro. This latter couple have several hurdles to jump in trying to marry. Marcellina, a housekeeper, is trying to force the much younger Figaro to marry her as penalty for an old debt which he cannot repay. And the Count is straying from his wife, making advances toward Susanna. It is here in the first act, as Figaro has been informed by his beloved that the Count has been making these overtures, that he expresses his fear and anger towards his master in a solo scene with the aria **Se vuol ballare, signor contino**. This highlight, one of the most memorable arias in the score, is a primary element in our understanding of Figaro's character.

To bring the Count back to the Countess, Figaro and Susanna plan with the Countess to send a note anonymously to the Count telling him falsely of a rendezvous between the Countess and a lover. Simultaneously, they plan a rendezvous between Susanna and the Count: the two women will disguise the young page Cherubino as a girl and send him in Susanna's stead. The Countess and Susanna dress the young Cherubino in women's clothes for their ruse, instructing the boy in how to effect a properly feminine manner. This scene, though, is interrupted by the Count, who suspects a liaison.

It is at the beginning of Act Three that the Count, having secured Susanna's promise to meet him in the garden, overhears her whisper to Figaro that they have been successful in their plot. The Count's aria **Vedrò mentr'io** acts as a counterpart to Figaro's **Se vuol ballare**, but this time it is the Count who is so angry at the thought of being the victim of a deception. In the ensuing action, the confusion mounts, especially for the unknowing Count, and it is finally revealed that Marcellina's long-lost son is none other than Figaro, whom she has been trying to claim in marriage! This of course eliminates one obstacle to the young couple's union. But the Countess has also arranged for Susanna to rendezvous with the Count, and the two women decide now to exchange identities to trick the Count into realizing his love for his wife. But it is Figaro who has misunderstood the intervening developments, and when he spies Susanna singing of her love, he mistakenly thinks she's singing for the Count rather than for himself.

In the end, all are happily reunited and the marriage proceeds to everyone's great joy. And *Le Nozze di Figaro*, with its deliciously serpentine plot, has emerged as one of the greatest operas of all time.

It was 30 years after *Figaro* that Rossini would pen an operatic version of its precursor, *Il Barbiere di Siviglia*, although there had previously been an opera by Paisiello on the subject. Rossini had originally titled his version *Almaviva, ossia l'inutile precauzione*, and the public, who loved this opera much more than Paisiello's, would not accept the new title and took it upon themselves to force the issue, resulting in its proper title of *Il Barbiere di Siviglia*.

The story takes us back to Seville, where the Barber Figaro helps Count Almaviva disguise himself in order to win the hand of the lovely Rosina, who is to be wedded to her guardian, Dr. Bartolo. But Bartolo's pal Don Basilio, who has discovered the arrival in Seville of the Count, sings the aria **La callunia è un venticello** in which he suggests spreading malicious rumors about the Count. In the ensuing madness, after which every possible complication is played out, the Count and Rosina are eventually married and Bartolo has no choice but to bless the couple's union, ending the opera on the happiest of notes.

It was in a much more somber vein that Verdi composed his *Simon Boccanegra*. He initially wrote it in Paris in 1856-57 having finished the unhappy process of composing *Les Vêpres Siciliennes (I Vespri Siciliani)*, using as librettists Francesco Maria Piave and Giuseppe Montanelli, basing it on Antonio Garcia Gutierrez's play of the same name. The public found its subject matter so depressing, not to mention confusing and incoherent, that it was a failure. Heavily criticized, it lay dormant for over twenty years until he was persuaded by Ricordi to revise it in 1880, this time collaborating with the excellent librettist Arrigo Boito. The changes were largely confined to the first act, where the second scene was completely scuttled and replaced. The second act was barely touched, and it is partially because of this resulting unevenness that it has become one of Verdi's most controversial works: though filled with brilliant music, it explores dark, unsettling themes and has a narrative whose inconsistency is the only possible compromise to the piece as a whole. Still, the opera's magnificent music, and its many great arias, outweigh its narrative problems and have kept it in the repertoire.

The opera begins with the death of Maria, daughter of Jacopo Fiesco, a Genovese nobleman who had confined her to the palace because she was the object of buccaneer Simon Boccanegra's affections and in fact had a child by him. In Fiesco's aria, **Il lacerato spirito**, the grieving father laments his daughter's death and puts a curse on Simon. This brilliantly foreboding aria, with its dirge-like plainchant quality, sets the tone for the brooding, dark quality of everything that is to come. Its undertones, beginning with surging low horns and then with *tremolando* strings, sets off his impassioned aria with great dignity and sadness.

Finally, from Puccini's *La Bohème* comes Colline's heartfelt expression of sadness, **Vecchia zimarra**. He and the other bohemians are trying to raise money for medical help as their friend Mimi approaches her death, and he sings this aria as he parts with his coat in a gesture of charity. As only Puccini could, this brilliant aria's pathos is effectively underscored with delicate woodwinds—flute, clarinet, oboe, and bassoon—and rhythmic *pizzicato* strings beneath, conveying simultaneously the sweetness of the emotion, and yet the gravity and sadness of what is to come. It is just this quality that has made *La Bohème* one of the most perfect creations in the entire repertoire.

—*Michael Norell*

Printed in Canada

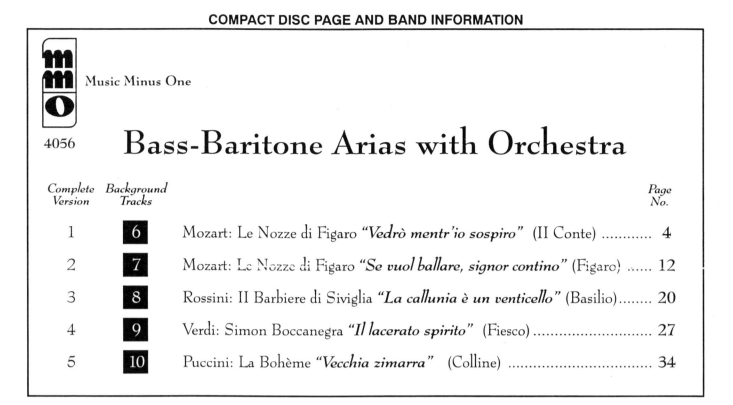

Music Minus One

4056

Bass-Baritone Arias with Orchestra

W.A.Mozart
Le Nozze di Figaro
Vedro mentr'io sospiro

Atto.III. Seguito della Scena III.

CONTE.

Hai già vinta la causa? cosa sento? in qual laccio ca_dea!

Orchestra

PRESTO. perfidi! io vo_glio, io voglio di tal modo pu_

_nirvi,.... a piacer mio la sen_tenza sarà...

ANDANTE. Ma s'ei pa_gasse la vecchia pretendente?

I.^{mo} TEMPO.

pagarla? in qual maniera?

CONTE

ALL? MAESTOSO.

Ve_

_drò mentr'io so_spi_ro,   fe _ li _ ce un ser _ vo   mio?

e un ben, che invan de_si_o,

ei pos_seder do_vrà?   Ve_drò per man d'a_more,   u_

-ni_ta a un vil og_get_to chi in me de_stò un af__fet_to, che

per me poi non ha, che per me poi non ha? Ve _

-dró,........mentr'io so_spi_ro,........fe _ li_ce un ser _ vo mi_o? e un

ben, che invan........de _ si _ o,......... ei pos _ se _ der do _ vrà? ve_

_drò per man d'a_mo_re u_ni_ta a un vil og_get_to chi in me de_sto un af_

fetto, che per me poi non ha, che per me poi non ha? ve

_drò? ve _ drò? ve _ drò? ve _ drò? Ah

ALL.º ASSAI

no, lasciar _ ti in _ pa _ ce non vo' questo con_ten _ to!

tu non na _ sce_sti au _ da_ce! tu non ha_sce _ sti au_da_ce! per

da _ _ re a me tor _ men _ to, e for _ se ancor per

ri _ dere, per ri _ dere di mia in _ fe _ li _ ci _ tà.

Già la spe _ ran _ za so _ la del _ le vendet _ te mi _ e que _

_ st'a _ ni _ ma con _ so _ la, e giu _ bi _ lar mi fa, e giu _ bi _

_lar, e giu_bi_lar mi fa. Ah.......che lasciarti in pace non

vo' que_sto con_tento! tu non na_sce_sti,au_da_ce, per

da___re a me tor_men_to; e for_se ancor per

ri_dere, per ri_dere di mia in_fe_li_ci_tà.

Già la spe_ranza so_la del_le ven_det_te mi_e que_

Mozart
Le Nozze di Figaro
Se vuol ballare

*Appoggiatura
Recommended

se - cre-ta am-ba-scia-tri - ce. Non sa - rà, non sa-rà, Fi - ga-ro il di - ce!

Allegretto

Se vuol bal - la - re, si - gnor con - ti - no, se vuol bal -

la - re, si - gnor con - ti - no, il chi - tar - ri - no le

suo - ne - rò, il chi - tar - ri - no le suo - ne -

14

rò, sì, le suo-ne-rò, sì, le suo-ne-rò.

Se vuol ve - ni - re

nel - la mia scuo - la, la ca - pri - o - la

le in - se - gne - rò. Se vuol ve-ni - re nel - la mia

scuo - la, la ca - pri - o - la le in - se - gne - rò, sì,

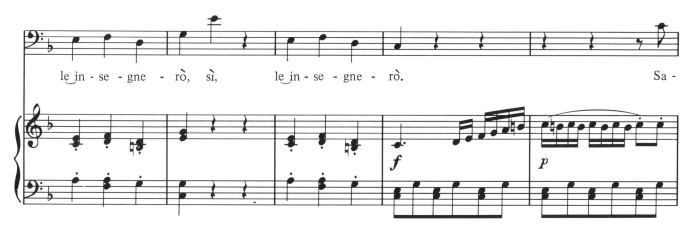

le in - se - gne - rò, sì, le in - se - gne - rò. Sa -

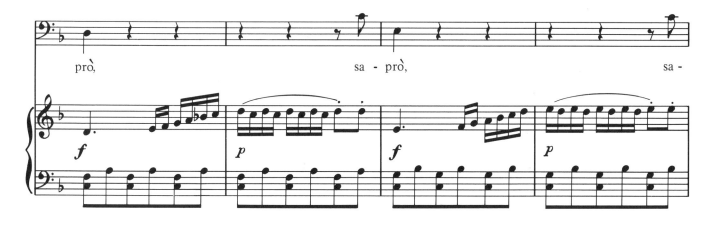

prò, sa - prò, sa -

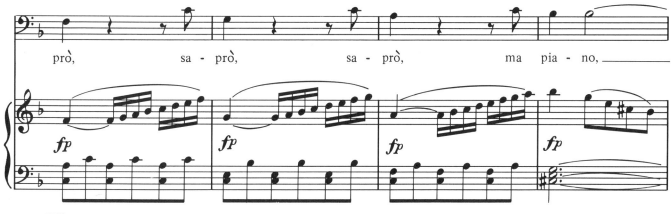

prò, sa - prò, sa - prò, ma pia - no, _____

pia - no, pia - no, pia - no, pia - no, pia - no, pia - no;

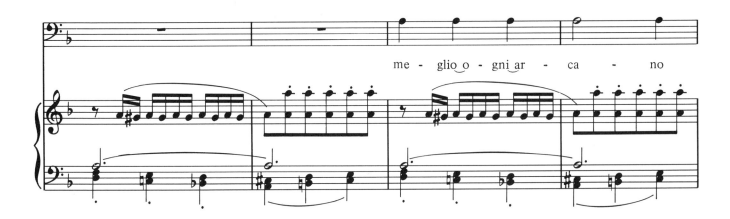

me - glio o - gni ar - ca - no

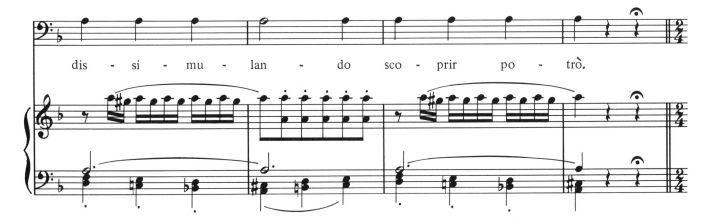

dis - si - mu - lan - do sco - prir po - trò.

Presto

L'ar - te scher - men - do, l'ar - te a - do - pran - do,

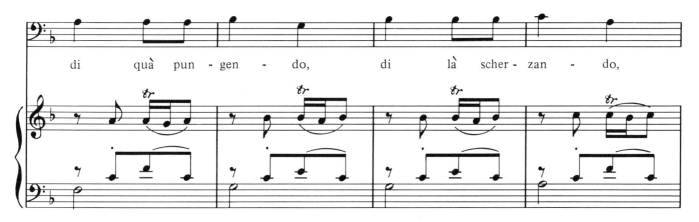

di quà pun - gen - do, di là scher - zan - do,

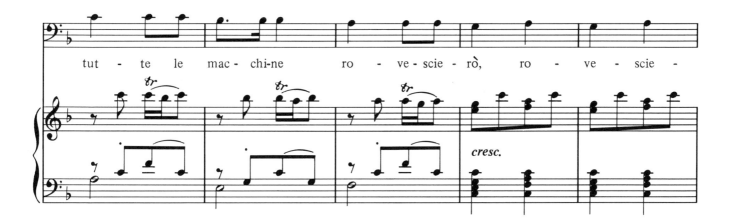

tut - te le mac - chi-ne ro - ve-scie - rò, ro - ve - scie -

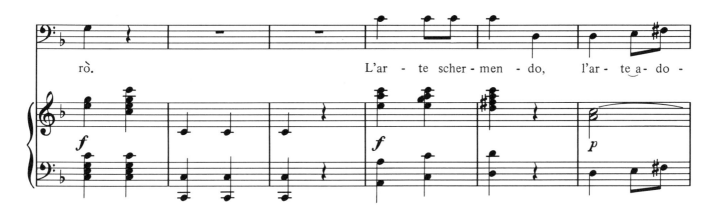

rò. L'ar - te scher-men - do, l'ar-te a-do -

pran - do, di quà pun - gen - do, di là scher - zan - do,

tut - te le mac - chi - ne ro - ve - scie - rò, tut - te le

mac - chi - ne ro - ve - scie - rò, tut - te le mac - chi - ne

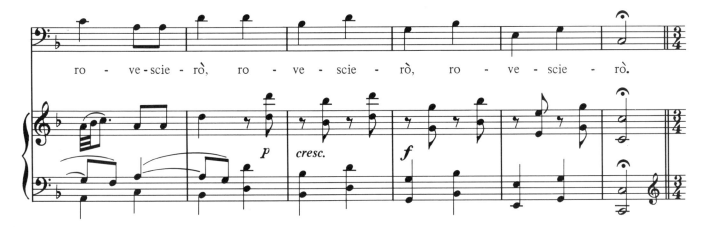

ro - ve - scie - rò, ro - ve - scie - rò, ro - ve - scie - rò.

[Tempo 1]

Se vuol bal - la - re, si - gnor con - ti - no,

se vuol bal - la - re, si - gnor con - ti - no,

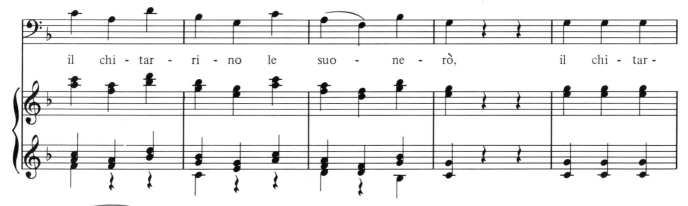

il chi - tar - ri - no le suo - ne - rò, il chi - tar -

ri - no le suo - ne - rò, sì, le suo - ne -

Presto

rò, sì, le suo - ne - rò.

Rossini
The Barber of Seville
Basilio's Aria

MMO 4056

che in-sen-si-bi-le, sot-ti-le, leg-ger-men-te, dol-ce-men-te In-co-

min-cia, in-co-min-cia a su-sur-rar. Pia-no

pia-no, ter-ra ter-ra,

sot-to vo-ce si-bi-

lan-do va scorren-do, va scor-ren-

do,   va ron-zan-do, va ron-zan - - do;   nel-l'o-rec-chie del-la

cresc.   *a poco*

gen-te   s'in-tro-du-ce, s'in-tro-du-ce de-stra-men-te, e le te-ste ed i cer-

cresc.

vel-li, e le te-ste ed i cer-vel-li fa stor-di-re, fa stor-di-re, fa stor-di-re e fa gon-

fiar.   Dal - la boc-ca fuo-ri u-

Str.

p

Brass

scendo   lo schiamaz-zo va cre-scen-do,

Cl.

cresc.

pren-de for- za a po-co a po-co, vo-la già di lo-co in

lo-co, sembra il tuo-no, la tempe-sta che nel sen del-la fo-re-sta va fischiando, bronto-

lan-do, e ti fa d'or-ror ge- lar. Al- la fin tra-boc-ca e scoppia, si pro-pa-ga, si rad-

dop-pia e pro-du-ce un'e-splo-sio-ne co-me un col-po di can-

no - ne, co-me un col-po di can-no - ne, un tre-muo-to, un tem-po-

ra - le, un tre-muo-to, un tempo-ra-le, un tremuoto, un tempo-ra-le che fa l'a-ria rim-bom-

bar, un tre-muo-to, un tempo-ra-le, un tre-muo-to, un tempo-ra-le, un tremuoto, un tempo-

ra - le che fa l'a-ria rim-bom-bar! E il me-

schi - no ca - lun - nia - to, av - vi - li - to, cal - pe - sta - to, sot - to il

pub - bli - co fla - gel - lo per gran sor - te va a cre-par. E il me-

schi - no ca - lun - nia - to, av - vi - li - to, cal - pe - sta - to, sot - to il pub - bli - co fla -

gel - lo_ per_ gran sor - te_ va a cre - par.

E il me - schi - no ca - lun - nia - to, av - vi - li - to, cal - pe -

sta - to, sot - to il pub - bli - co_ fla - gel - lo_ per gran

sor - te_ va a cre - par. E il me - schi - no ca - lun - nia - to, av - vi -

Verdi
Simon Boccanegra
Fiesco's Aria

(Varie persone escono dal palazzo, e
traversando mestamente la piazza
a'allentanano)

F

me................................

non la ve-drem mai più!

non la ve-drem mai più!

non la ve-drem mai più!

S
pp

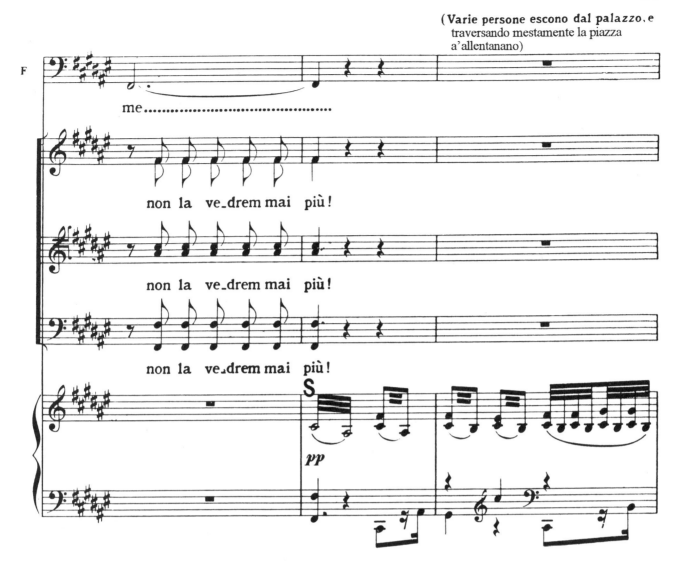

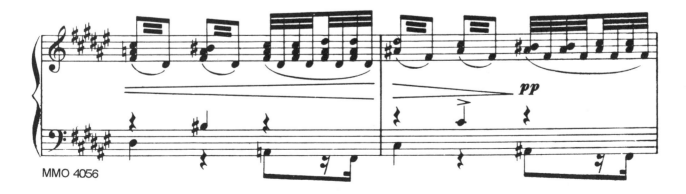

pp

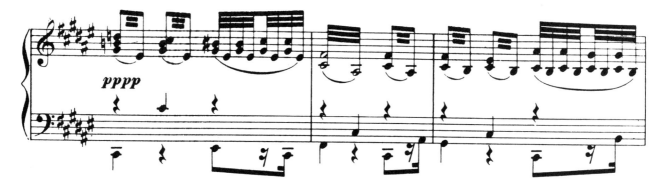

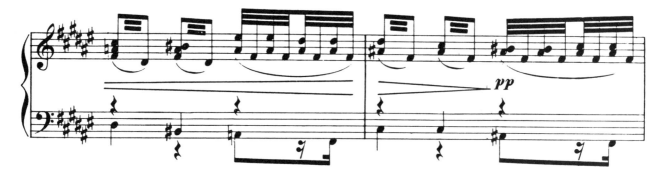

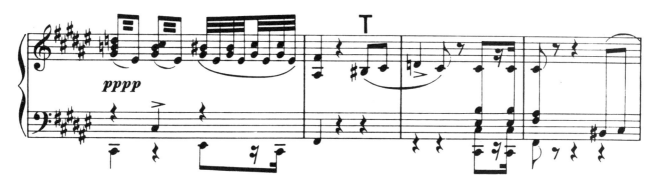

Puccini
La Boheme
Vecchia zimarra, senti

COLLINE:

Vec - chia zi - mar - ra, sen - ti, io re-sto al pian, tu a

scen - de-re il sa-cro mon-te or de - vi. Le mie gra - zie ri - ce-vi.

Mai non cur-va - sti il lo - go-ro dor-so ai ric-chi ed ai po-ten - ti.

MMO Compact Disc Catalog

BROADWAY

CLARINET

PIANO

PIANO - FOUR HANDS

VIOLIN

MMO Music Group • 50 Executive Boulevard, Elmsford, New York 10523, 1-(800) 669-7464
Website: www. minusone.com • E-mail: mmomus@aol.com

MMO Compact Disc Catalog

- BRAHMS CONCERTO IN D OP. 77 ... MMO CD 3108
- CHAUSSON POEME, SCHUBERT RONDO ... MMO CD 3109
- LALO SYMPHONIE ESPAGNOLE ... MMO CD 3110
- MOZART CONCERTO IN D K.218, VIVALDI CON. AM OP.3 NO.6 ... MMO CD 3111
- MOZART CONCERTO IN A K.219 ... MMO CD 3112
- WIENIAWSKI CON. IN D. SARASATE ZIGEUNERWEISEN ... MMO CD 3113
- VIOTTI CONCERTO NO. 22 IN A MINOR ... MMO CD 3114
- BEETHOVEN 2 ROMANCES, SONATA NO. 5 IN F "SPRING SONATA" ... MMO CD 3115
- SAINT-SAENS INTRODUCTION & RONDO,
- MOZART SERENADE K. 204, ADAGIO K.261 ... MMO CD 3116
- BEETHOVEN CONCERTO IN D OP. 61(2 CD SET) ... MMO CD 3117
- THE CONCERTMASTER - Orchestral Excerpts ... MMO CD 3118
- AIR ON A G STRING Favorite Encores with Orchestra Easy Medium ... MMO CD 3119
- CONCERT PIECES FOR THE SERIOUS VIOLINIST Easy Medium ... MMO CD 3120
- 18TH CENTURY VIOLIN PIECES ... MMO CD 3121
- ORCHESTRAL FAVORITES - Volume 1 - Easy Level ... MMO CD 3122
- ORCHESTRAL FAVORITES - Volume 2 - Medium Level ... MMO CD 3123
- ORCHESTRAL FAVORITES - Volume 3 - Med to Difficult Level ... MMO CD 3124
- THE THREE B'S BACH/BEETHOVEN/BRAHMS ... MMO CD 3125
- VIVALDI: VIOLIN CONCERTOS ... MMO CD 3126
- VIVALDI-THE FOUR SEASONS (2 CD Set) ... MMO CD 3127
- VIVALDI Concerto in Eb, Op. 8, No. 5. ALBINONI Concerto in A ... MMO CD 3128
- VIVALDI Concerto in E, Op. 3, No. 12. Concerto in C Op. 8, No.6 "Il Piacere" MMO CD 3129
- SCHUBERT Three Sonatinas ... MMO CD 3130
- HAYDN String Quartet Op. 76 No. 1 ... MMO CD 3131
- HAYDN String Quartet Op. 76 No. 2 ... MMO CD 3132
- HAYDN String Quartet Op. 76 No. 3 "Emperor" ... MMO CD 3133
- HAYDN String Quartet Op. 76 No. 4 "Sunrise" ... MMO CD 3134
- HAYDN String Quartet Op. 76 No. 5 ... MMO CD 3135
- HAYDN String Quartet Op. 76 No. 6 ... MMO CD 3136
- BEAUTIFUL MUSIC FOR TWO VIOLINS 1st position, vol. 1 ... MMO CD 3137★
- BEAUTIFUL MUSIC FOR TWO VIOLINS 2nd position, vol. 2 ... MMO CD 3138★
- BEAUTIFUL MUSIC FOR TWO VIOLINS 3rd position, vol. 3 ... MMO CD 3139★
- BEAUTIFUL MUSIC FOR TWO VIOLINS 1st, 2nd, 3rd position, vol. 4 ... MMO CD 3140★

★Lovely folk tunes and selections from the classics, chosen for their melodic beauty and technical value. They have been skillfully transcribed and edited by Samuel Applebaum, one of America's foremost teachers.

- HEART OF THE VIOLIN CONCERTO ... MMO CD 3141
- TEACHER'S PARTNER Basic Violin Studies 1st year ... MMO CD 3142
- DVORAK STRING TRIO "Terzetto", OP. 74 2 violins/viola ... MMO CD 3143
- SIBELIUS: Concerto in D minor, Op. 47 ... MMO CD 3144
- THEMES FROM THE MAJOR VIOLIN CONCERTI ... MMO CD 3145
- STRAVINSKY: L'HISTOIRE DU SOLDAT ... MMO CD 3146
- RAVEL: PIANO TRIO MINUS VIOLIN ... MMO CD 3147
- GREAT VIOLIN MOMENTS ... MMO CD 3148
- RAGTIME STRING QUARTETS The Zinn String Quartet ... MMO CD 3151
- SCHUMANN: Piano Trio in D minor, Opus 63 ... MMO CD 3152
- BEETHOVEN: Trio No. 8 & Trio No. 11, "Kakadu" Variations ... MMO CD 3153
- SCHUBERT: Piano Trio in Bb Major, Opus 99 Minus Violin (2 CD Set) ... MMO CD 3154
- SCHUBERT: Piano Trio in Eb Major, Opus 100 Minus Violin (2 CD Set) ... MMO CD 3155
- BEETHOVEN: STRING QUARTET in A minor, Opus 132 (2 CD Set) ... MMO CD 3156
- DVORAK QUINTET in A major, Opus 81 Minus Violin ... MMO CD 3157
- BEETHOVEN: STRING QTS No. 1 in F major & No. 4 in C minor, Opus 18 ... MMO CD 3158
- HAYDN Three Trios with Piano & Cello ... MMO CD 3159
- MOZART: CONCERTO NO. 3 FOR VIOLIN AND ORCHESTRA. ... MMO CD 3160
- MISCHA ELMAN FAVORITE ENCORES. ... MMO CD 3162
- MISCHA ELMAN CONCERT FAVORITES ... MMO CD 3163
- JASCHA HEIFETZ FAVORITE ENCORES. ... MMO CD 3164
- FRITZ KREISLER FAVORITE ENCORES ... MMO CD 3165

GUITAR

- BOCCHERINI Quintet No. 4 in D "Fandango" ... MMO CD 3601
- GIULIANI Quintet in A Op. 65 ... MMO CD 3602
- CLASSICAL GUITAR DUETS ... MMO CD 3603
- RENAISSANCE & BAROQUE GUITAR DUETS ... MMO CD 3604
- CLASSICAL & ROMANTIC GUITAR DUETS ... MMO CD 3605
- GUITAR AND FLUTE DUETS Volume 1 ... MMO CD 3606
- GUITAR AND FLUTE DUETS Volume 2 ... MMO CD 3607
- BLUEGRASS GUITAR ... MMO CD 3608
- GEORGE BARNES GUITAR METHOD Lessons from a Master ... MMO CD 3609
- HOW TO PLAY FOLK GUITAR 2 CD Set ... MMO CD 3610
- FAVORITE FOLKS SONGS FOR GUITAR ... MMO CD 3611
- FOR GUITARS ONLY! Jimmy Raney Small Band Arrangements ... MMO CD 3612
- TEN DUETS FOR TWO GUITARS Geo. Barnes/Carl Kress ... MMO CD 3613
- PLAY THE BLUES GUITAR A Dick Weissman Method ... MMO CD 3614
- ORCHESTRAL GEMS FOR CLASSICAL GUITAR ... MMO CD 3615

FLUTE

- MOZART Concerto No. 2 in D, QUANTZ Concerto in G ... MMO CD 3300
- MOZART Concerto in G K.313 ... MMO CD 3301
- BACH Suite No. 2 in B Minor ... MMO CD 3302
- BOCCHERINI Concerto in D, VIVALDI Concerto in G Minor "La Notte",
- MOZART Andante for Strings ... MMO CD 3303
- HAYDN Divertimento, VIVALDI Concerto in D Op. 10 No. 3 "Bullfinch",
- FREDERICK THE GREAT Concerto in C ... MMO CD 3304
- VIVALDI Conc. in F; TELEMANN Conc. in D; LECLAIR Conc. in C ... MMO CD 3305
- BACH Brandenburg No. 2 in F, HAYDN Concerto in D ... MMO CD 3306
- BACH Triple Concerto, VIVALDI Concerto in D Minor ... MMO CD 3307
- MOZART Quartet in F, STAMITZ Quartet in F ... MMO CD 3308
- HAYDN 4 London Trios for 2 Flutes & Cello ... MMO CD 3309
- BACH Brandenburg Concerti Nos. 4 & 5 ... MMO CD 3310
- MOZART 3 Flute Quartets in D, A and C ... MMO CD 3311
- TELEMANN Suite in A Minor, GLUCK Scene from 'Orpheus',
- PERGOLESI Concerto in G (2 CD Set) ... MMO CD 3312
- FLUTE SONG: Easy Familiar Classics ... MMO CD 3313
- VIVALDI Concerti In D, G, and F ... MMO CD 3314
- VIVALDI Concerti in A Minor, G, and D ... MMO CD 3315
- EASY FLUTE SOLOS Beginning Students Volume 1 ... MMO CD 3316
- EASY FLUTE SOLOS Beginning Students Volume 2 ... MMO CD 3317
- EASY JAZZ DUETS Student Level ... MMO CD 3318
- FLUTE & GUITAR DUETS Volume 1 ... MMO CD 3319
- FLUTE & GUITAR DUETS Volume 2 ... MMO CD 3320
- BEGINNING CONTEST SOLOS Murray Panitz ... MMO CD 3321
- BEGINNING CONTEST SOLOS Donald Peck ... MMO CD 3322
- INTERMEDIATE CONTEST SOLOS Julius Baker ... MMO CD 3323
- INTERMEDIATE CONTEST SOLOS Donald Peck ... MMO CD 3324
- ADVANCED CONTEST SOLOS Murray Panitz ... MMO CD 3325
- ADVANCED CONTEST SOLOS Julius Baker ... MMO CD 3326
- INTERMEDIATE CONTEST SOLOS Donald Peck ... MMO CD 3327
- ADVANCED CONTEST SOLOS Murray Panitz ... MMO CD 3328
- ADVANCED CONTEST SOLOS Julius Baker ... MMO CD 3329
- BEGINNING CONTEST SOLOS Doriot Anthony Dwyer ... MMO CD 3330
- INTERMEDIATE CONTEST SOLOS Doriot Anthony Dwyer ... MMO CD 3331
- ADVANCED CONTEST SOLOS Doriot Anthony Dwyer ... MMO CD 3332
- FIRST CHAIR SOLOS with Orchestral Accompaniment ... MMO CD 3333
- TEACHER'S PARTNER Basic Flute Studies 1st year ... MMO CD 3334
- THE JOY OF WOODWIND MUSIC ... MMO CD 3335
- JEWELS FOR WOODWIND QUINTET ... MMO CD 3336
- TELEMANN TRIO IN F/Bb MAJOR/HANDEL SON.#3 IN C MAJOR ... MMO CD 3340
- MARCELLO/TELEMANN/HANDEL SONATAS IN F MAJOR ... MMO CD 3341
- BOLLING: SUITE FOR FLUTE/JAZZ PIANO TRIO ... MMO CD 3342
- HANDEL / TELEMANN SIX SONATAS 2 CD Set ... MMO CD 3343
- BACH SONATA NO. 1 in B MINOR/KUHLAU E MINOR DUET (2 CD set) ... MMO CD 3344
- KUHLAU TRIO in Eb MAJOR/BACH Eb AND A MAJOR SONATA (2 CD set) .. MMO CD 3345
- PEPUSCH SONATA IN C / TELEMANN SONATA IN Cm ... MMO CD 3346
- QUANTZ TRIO SONATA IN Cm / BACH GIGUE / ABEL SON. 2 IN F ... MMO CD 3347
- TELEMANN CONCERTO NO. 1 IN D / CORRETTE SONATA IN E MINOR ... MMO CD 3348
- TELEMANN TRIO IN F / Bb MAJOR / HANDEL SON. #3 IN C MAJOR ... MMO CD 3349
- MARCELLO / TELEMANN / HANDEL SONATAS IN F MAJOR ... MMO CD 3350
- CONCERT BAND FAVORITES WITH ORCHESTRA ... MMO CD 3351
- BAND-AIDS CONCERT BAND FAVORITES WITH ORCHESTRA ... MMO CD 3352
- UNSUNG HERO George Roberts ... MMO CD 3353
- WORLD FAVORITES Student Editions, 41 Easy Selections (1st-2nd year) ... MMO CD 3354
- CLASSIC THEMES Student Editions, 27 Easy Songs (2nd-3rd year) ... MMO CD 3355

RECORDER

- PLAYING THE RECORDER Folk Songs of Many Nations ... MMO CD 3337
- LET'S PLAY THE RECORDER Beginning Children's Method ... MMO CD 3338
- YOU CAN PLAY THE RECORDER Beginning Adult Method ... MMO CD 3339

FRENCH HORN

- MOZART: Concerti No. 2 & No. 3 in Eb. K. 417 & 447 ... MMO CD 3501
- BAROQUE BRASS AND BEYOND ... MMO CD 3502
- MUSIC FOR BRASS ENSEMBLE ... MMO CD 3503
- MOZART: Sonatas for Two Horns ... MMO CD 3504
- BEETHOVEN: QUINTET FOR FRENCH HORN in Eb Major, Opus 16 ... MMO CD 3505
- MOZART: QUINTET FOR FRENCH HORN in Eb, K.452 ... MMO CD 3506
- BEGINNING CONTEST SOLOS Mason Jones ... MMO CD 3511
- BEGINNING CONTEST SOLOS Myron Bloom ... MMO CD 3512
- INTERMEDIATE CONTEST SOLOS Dale Clevenger ... MMO CD 3513
- INTERMEDIATE CONTEST SOLOS Mason Jones ... MMO CD 3514
- ADVANCED CONTEST SOLOS Myron Bloom ... MMO CD 3515
- ADVANCED CONTEST SOLOS Dale Clevenger ... MMO CD 3516
- INTERMEDIATE CONTEST SOLOS Mason Jones ... MMO CD 3517
- ADVANCED CONTEST SOLOS Myron Bloom ... MMO CD 3518
- INTERMEDIATE CONTEST SOLOS Dale Clevenger ... MMO CD 3519
- FRENCH HORN WOODWIND MUSIC ... MMO CD 3520
- MASTERPIECES FOR WOODWIND QUINTET ... MMO CD 3521
- FRENCH HORN UP FRONT BRASS QUINTETS ... MMO CD 3522
- HORN OF PLENTY BRASS QUINTETS ... MMO CD 3523
- BAND-AIDS CONCERT BAND FAVORITES WITH ORCHESTRA ... MMO CD 3524

MMO Music Group • 50 Executive Boulevard, Elmsford, New York 10523, 1-(800) 669-7464
Website: www. minusone.com • E-mail: mmomus@aol.com

MMO Compact Disc Catalog

TRUMPET

THREE CONCERTI: HAYDN, TELEMANN, FASCH	MMO CD 3801
TRUMPET SOLOS Student Level Volume 1	MMO CD 3802
TRUMPET SOLOS Student Level Volume 2	MMO CD 3803
EASY JAZZ DUETS Student Level	MMO CD 3804
MUSIC FOR BRASS ENSEMBLE Brass Quintets	MMO CD 3805
FIRST CHAIR TRUMPET SOLOS with Orchestral Accompaniment	MMO CD 3806
THE ART OF THE SOLO TRUMPET with Orchestral Accompaniment	MMO CD 3807
BAROQUE BRASS AND BEYOND Brass Quintets	MMO CD 3808
THE COMPLETE ARBAN DUETS all of the classic studies	MMO CD 3809
SOUSA MARCHES PLUS BEETHOVEN, BERLIOZ, STRAUSS	MMO CD 3810
BEGINNING CONTEST SOLOS Gerard Schwarz	MMO CD 3811
BEGINNING CONTEST SOLOS Armando Ghitalla	MMO CD 3812
INTERMEDIATE CONTEST SOLOS Robert Nagel, Soloist	MMO CD 3813
INTERMEDIATE CONTEST SOLOS Gerard Schwarz	MMO CD 3814
ADVANCED CONTEST SOLOS Robert Nagel, Soloist	MMO CD 3815
CONTEST SOLOS Armando Ghitalla	MMO CD 3816
INTERMEDIATE CONTEST SOLOS Gerard Schwarz	MMO CD 3817
ADVANCED CONTEST SOLOS Robert Nagel, Soloist	MMO CD 3818
ADVANCED CONTEST SOLOS Armando Ghilalla	MMO CD 3819
BEGINNING CONTEST SOLOS Raymond Crisara	MMO CD 3820
BEGINNING CONTEST SOLOS Raymond Crisara	MMO CD 3821
INTERMEDIATE CONTEST SOLOS Raymond Crisara	MMO CD 3822
TEACHER'S PARTNER Basic Trumpet Studies 1st year	MMO CD 3823
TWENTY DIXIELAND CLASSICS	MMO CD 3824
TWENTY RHYTHM BACKGROUNDS TO STANDARDS	MMO CD 3825
FROM DIXIE TO SWING	MMO CD 3826
TRUMPET PIECES BRASS QUINTETS	MMO CD 3827
MODERN BRASS QUINTETS	MMO CD 3828
WHEN JAZZ WAS YOUNG The Bob Wilber All Stars	MMO CD 3829
CLASSIC TRUMPET SELECTIONS WITH PIANO	MMO CD 3830
CONCERT BAND FAVORITES WITH ORCHESTRA	MMO CD 3831
BAND-AIDS CONCERT BAND FAVORITES WITH ORCHESTRA	MMO CD 3832
BRASS TRAX The Trumpet Artistry Of David O'Neill	MMO CD 3833
TRUMPET TRIUMPHANT The Further Adventures Of David O'Neill	MMO CD 3834
WORLD FAVORITES Student Editions, 41 Easy Selections (1st-2nd year)	MMO CD 3836
CLASSIC THEMES Student Editions, 27 Easy Songs (2nd-3rd year)	MMO CD 3837
6 BANDS ON A HOT TIN ROOF New Swing for Trumpet	MMO CD 3838
STRAVINSKY: L'HISTOIRE DU SOLDAT	MMO CD 3835
12 CLASSIC JAZZ STANDARDS Bb/Eb/Bass Clef	MMO CD 7010
12 MORE CLASSIC JAZZ STANDARDS Bb/Eb/Bass Clef	MMO CD 7011

TROMBONE

TROMBONE SOLOS Student Level Volume 1	MMO CD 3901
TROMBONE SOLOS Student Level Volume 2	MMO CD 3902
EASY JAZZ DUETS Student Level	MMO CD 3903
BAROQUE BRASS & BEYOND Brass Quintets	MMO CD 3904
MUSIC FOR BRASS ENSEMBLE Brass Quintets	MMO CD 3905
UNSUNG HERO George Roberts	MMO CD 3906
BIG BAND BALLADS George Roberts	MMO CD 3907
STRAVINSKY: L'HISTOIRE DU SOLDAT	MMO CD 3908
CLASSICAL TROMBONE SOLOS	MMO CD 3909
JAZZ STANDARDS WITH STRINGS (2 CD Set)	MMO CD 3910
BEGINNING CONTEST SOLOS Per Brevig	MMO CD 3911
BEGINNING CONTEST SOLOS Jay Friedman	MMO CD 3912
INTERMEDIATE CONTEST SOLOS Keith Brown, Professor, Indiana U.	MMO CD 3913
INTERMEDIATE CONTEST SOLOS Jay Friedman	MMO CD 3914
ADVANCED CONTEST SOLOS Keith Brown, Professor, Indiana University	MMO CD 3915
ADVANCED CONTEST SOLOS Per Brevig	MMO CD 3916
ADVANCED CONTEST SOLOS Keith Brown, Professor, Indiana University	MMO CD 3917
ADVANCED CONTEST SOLOS Jay Friedman	MMO CD 3918
ADVANCED CONTEST SOLOS Per Brevig	MMO CD 3919
TEACHER'S PARTNER Basic Trombone Studies 1st year	MMO CD 3920
TWENTY DIXIELAND CLASSICS	MMO CD 3924
TWENTY RHYTHM BACKGROUNDS TO STANDARDS	MMO CD 3925
FROM DIXIE TO SWING	MMO CD 3926
STICKS & BONES BRASS QUINTETS	MMO CD 3927
FOR TROMBONES ONLY MORE BRASS QUINTETS	MMO CD 3928
POPULAR CONCERT FAVORITES The Stuttgart Festival Band	MMO CD 3929
BAND-AIDS CONCERT BAND FAVORITES WITH ORCHESTRA	MMO CD 3930
WORLD FAVORITES Student Editions, 41 Easy Selections (1st-2nd year)	MMO CD 3931
CLASSIC THEMES Student Editions, 27 Easy Songs (2nd-3rd year)	MMO CD 3932
12 CLASSIC JAZZ STANDARDS Bb/Eb/Bass Clef	MMO CD 7010
12 MORE CLASSIC JAZZ STANDARDS Bb/Eb/Bass Clef	MMO CD 7011

TENOR SAXOPHONE

TENOR SAXOPHONE SOLOS Student Edition Volume 1	MMO CD 4201
TENOR SAXOPHONE SOLOS Student Edition Volume 2	MMO CD 4202
EASY JAZZ DUETS FOR TENOR SAXOPHONE	MMO CD 4203
FOR SAXES ONLY Arranged by Bob Wilber	MMO CD 4204
BLUES FUSION FOR SAXOPHONE	MMO CD 4205
JOBIM BRAZILIAN BOSSA NOVAS with STRINGS	MMO CD 4206
TWENTY DIXIE CLASSICS	MMO CD 4207
TWENTY RHYTHM BACKGROUNDS TO STANDARDS	MMO CD 4208
PLAY LEAD IN A SAX SECTION	MMO CD 4209
DAYS OF WINE & ROSES Sax Section Minus You	MMO CD 4210
FRENCH & AMERICAN SAXOPHONE QUARTETS	MMO CD 4211
CONCERT BAND FAVORITES WITH ORCHESTRA	MMO CD 4212
BAND AIDS CONCERT BAND FAVORITES	MMO CD 4213
JAZZ JAM FOR TENOR (2 CD Set)	MMO CD 4214
6 BANDS ON A HOT TIN ROOF New Swing for Saxophone	MMO CD 4215
12 CLASSIC JAZZ STANDARDS Bb/Eb/Bass Clef	MMO CD 7010
12 MORE CLASSIC JAZZ STANDARDS Bb/Eb/Bass Clef	MMO CD 7011

CELLO

DVORAK Concerto in B Minor Op. 104 (2 CD Set)	MMO CD 3701
C.P.E. BACH Concerto in A Minor	MMO CD 3702
BOCCHERINI Concerto in Bb, BRUCH Kol Nidrei	MMO CD 3703
TEN PIECES FOR CELLO	MMO CD 3704
SCHUMANN Concerto in Am & Other Selections	MMO CD 3705
CLAUDE BOLLING Suite For Cello & Jazz Piano Trio	MMO CD 3706
RAVEL: PIANO TRIO MINUS CELLO	MMO CD 3707
RAGTIME STRING QUARTETS	MMO CD 3708
SCHUMANN: Piano Trio in D Minor, Opus 63	MMO CD 3709
BEETHOVEN: Piano Trio For Cello	MMO CD 3710
SCHUBERT: Piano Trio in Bb Major, Opus 99 Minus Cello (2 CD Set)	MMO CD 3711
SCHUBERT: Piano Trio in Eb Major, Opus 100 Minus Cello (2 CD Set)	MMO CD 3712
BEETHOVEN: STRING QUARTET in A minor, Opus 132 (2 CD Set)	MMO CD 3713
DVORAK QUINTET in A Major, Opus 81 Minus Cello	MMO CD 3714

OBOE

ALBINONI Concerti in Bb, Op. 7 No. 3, No. 6, D. Op. 9 No. 2 in Dm	MMO CD 3400
TELEMANN Conc. in Fm; HANDEL Conc. in Bb; VIVALDI Conc.in Dm	MMO CD 3401
MOZART Quartet in F K.370, STAMITZ Quartet in F Op. 8 No. 3	MMO CD 3402
BACH Brandenburg Concerto No. 2, Telemann Con. in Am	MMO CD 3403
CLASSIC SOLOS FOR OBOE Delia Montenegro, Soloist	MMO CD 3404
MASTERPIECES FOR WOODWIND QUINTET	MMO CD 3405
THE JOY OF WOODWIND QUINTETS	MMO CD 3406
PEPUSCH SONATAS IN C/TELEMANN SONATA IN Cm	MMO CD 3407
QUANTZ TRIO SONATA IN Cm/BACH GIGUE/ABEL SONATAS IN F	MMO CD 3408
BEETHOVEN: QUINTET FOR OBOE in Eb, Opus 16	MMO CD 3409

ALTO SAXOPHONE

ALTO SAXOPHONE SOLOS Student Edition Volume 1	MMO CD 4101
ALTO SAXOPHONE SOLOS Student Edition Volume 2.	MMO CD 4102
EASY JAZZ DUETS FOR ALTO SAXOPHONE	MMO CD 4103
FOR SAXES ONLY Arranged Bob Wilber	MMO CD 4104
JOBIM BRAZILIAN BOSSA NOVAS with STRINGS	MMO CD 4106
UNSUNG HEROES FOR ALTO SAXOPHONE	MMO CD 4107
BEGINNING CONTEST SOLOS Paul Brodie, Canadian Soloist	MMO CD 4111
BEGINNING CONTEST SOLOS Vincent Abato	MMO CD 4112
INTERMEDIATE CONTEST SOLOS Paul Brodie, Canadian Soloist	MMO CD 4113
INTERMEDIATE CONTEST SOLOS Vincent Abato	MMO CD 4114
ADVANCED CONTEST SOLOS Paul Brodie. Canadian Soloist	MMO CD 4115
ADVANCED CONTEST SOLOS Vincent Abato	MMO CD 4116
ADVANCED CONTEST SOLOS Paul Brodie, Canadian Soloist	MMO CD 4117
Basic Studies for Alto Sax TEACHER'S PARTNER 1st year level	MMO CD 4119
ADVANCED CONTEST SOLOS Vincent Abato	MMO CD 4118
PLAY LEAD IN A SAX SECTION	MMO CD 4120
DAYS OF WINE & ROSES/SENSUAL SAX	MMO CD 4121
TWENTY DIXIELAND CLASSICS	MMO CD 4124
TWENTY RHYTHM BACKGROUNDS TO STANDARDS	MMO CD 4125
CONCERT BAND FAVORITES WITH ORCHESTRA	MMO CD 4126
BAND AIDS CONCERT BAND FAVORITES	MMO CD 4127
MUSIC FOR SAXOPHONE QUARTET	MMO CD 4128
WORLD FAVORITES Student Editions, 41 Easy Selections (1st-2nd year)	MMO CD 4129
CLASSIC THEMES Student Editions, 27 Easy Songs (2nd-3rd year)	MMO CD 4130
12 CLASSIC JAZZ STANDARDS Bb/Eb/Bass Clef	MMO CD 7010
12 MORE CLASSIC JAZZ STANDARDS Bb/Eb/Bass Clef	MMO CD 7011

SOPRANO SAXOPHONE

FRENCH & AMERICAN SAXOPHONE QUARTETS	MMO CD 4801
12 CLASSIC JAZZ STANDARDS Bb/Eb/Bass Clef	MMO CD 7010
12 MORE CLASSIC JAZZ STANDARDS Bb/Eb/Bass Clef	MMO CD 7011

MMO Music Group • 50 Executive Boulevard, Elmsford, New York 10523, 1-(800) 669-7464
Website: www. minusone.com • E-mail: mmomus@aol.com

Music Minus One Vocal Recordings

SCHUBERT GERMAN LIEDER - High Voice, Volume 1
....MMO CD 4001
SCHUBERT GERMAN LIEDER - Low Voice, Volume 1
....MMO CD 4002
SCHUBERT GERMAN LIEDER - High Voice, Volume 2
....MMO CD 4003
SCHUBERT GERMAN LIEDER - Low Voice, Vol. 2
....MMO CD 4004
BRAHMS GERMAN LIEDER - High Voice..............MMO CD 4005
BRAHMS GERMAN LIEDER - Low Voice ....MMO CD 4006
EVERYBODY'S FAVORITE SONGS - High Voice, Vol. 1
....MMO CD 4007
EVERYBODY'S FAVORITE SONGS - Low Voice, Vol. 1 .
....MMO CD 4008
EVERYBODY'S FAVORITE SONGS - High Voice, Vol. 2
....MMO CD 4009
EVERYBODY'S FAVORITE SONGS - Low Voice, Vol. 2 .
....MMO CD 4010
17th/18th CENT. ITALIAN SONGS - High Voice, Vol. 1
....MMO CD 4011
17th/18th CENT. ITALIAN SONGS - Low Voice, Vol. 1
....MMO CD 4012
17th/18th CENT. ITALIAN SONGS - High Voice, Vol. 2 ..MMO CD 4013
17th/18th CENT. ITALIAN SONGS - Low Voice, Vol. 2 .....MMO CD 4014
FAMOUS SOPRANO ARIAS ....MMO CD 4015
FAMOUS MEZZO-SOPRANO ARIAS ....MMO CD 4016
FAMOUS TENOR ARIAS ....MMO CD 4017
FAMOUS BARITONE ARIAS ....MMO CD 4018
FAMOUS BASS ARIAS...MMO CD 4019
WOLF GERMAN LIEDER FOR HIGH VOICE ....MMO CD 4020
WOLF GERMAN LIEDER FOR LOW VOICE ....MMO CD 4021
STRAUSS GERMAN LIEDER FOR HIGH VOICE....MMO CD 4022
STRAUSS GERMAN LIEDER FOR LOW VOICE .....MMO CD 4023
SCHUMANN GERMAN LIEDER FOR HIGH VOICE ....MMO CD 4024
SCHUMANN GERMAN LIEDER FOR LOW VOICE ....MMO CD 4025
MOZART ARIAS FOR SOPRANO ....MMO CD 4026
VERDI ARIAS FOR SOPRANO ....MMO CD 4027
ITALIAN ARIAS FOR SOPRANO ....MMO CD 4028
FRENCH ARIAS FOR SOPRANO....................................MMO CD 4029
ORATORIO ARIAS FOR SOPRANO ....MMO CD 4030
ORATORIO ARIAS FOR ALTO ....MMO CD 4031
ORATORIO ARIAS FOR TENOR ....MMO CD 4032
ORATORIO ARIAS FOR BASS ....MMO CD 4033
BEGINNING SOPRANO SOLOS Kate Hurney ....MMO CD 4041
INTERMEDIATE SOPRANO SOLOS Kate Hurney....MMO CD 4042
BEGINNING MEZZO SOPRANO SOLOS F. Kittelson ......MMO CD 4043
INTERMEDIATE MEZZO SOPRANO SOLOS F. Kittelson ....MMO CD 4044
ADVANCED MEZZO SOPRANO SOLOS F. Kittelson ......MMO CD 4045
BEGINNING CONTRALTO SOLOS Carline Ray ....MMO CD 4046
BEGINNING TENOR SOLOS George Shirley ....MMO CD 4047
INTERMEDIATE TENOR SOLOS George Shirley .....MMO CD 4048
ADVANCED TENOR SOLOS George Shirley ....MMO CD 4049
TWELVE CLASSIC VOCAL STANDARDS, VOL.1 .....MMO CD 4050
TWELVE CLASSIC VOCAL STANDARDS, VOL.2 .....MMO CD 4051
SOPRANO OPERA ARIAS WITH ORCHESTRA ....MMO CD 4052
PUCCINI ARIAS FOR SOPRANO WITH ORCHESTRA . ...MMO CD 4053
SOPRANO OPERA ARIAS WITH ORCHESTRA ....MMO CD 4054
VERDI ARIAS FOR MEZZO-SOPRANO WITH ORCHESTRA ......MMO CD 4055
BASS-BARITONE ARIAS WITH ORCHESTRA ....MMO CD 4056
TENOR OPERA ARIAS WITH ORCHESTRA ....MMO CD 4057
SOPRANO OPERA ARIAS WITH ORCHESTRA ....MMO CD 4058

music minus one bass-baritone

4056

BASS-BARITONE ARIAS *with Orchestra*

MOZART: Le Nozze Di Figaro -Conte- *"Vedrò mentr'io sospiro"*
MOZART: Le Nozze Di Figaro -Figaro- *"Se vuol ballare"*
ROSSINI: The Barber of Seville -Basilio- *Aria*
VERDI: Simon Boccanegra -Fiesco- *Aria*
PUCCINI: La Boheme -Colline- *Aria*

MMO Music Group • 50 Executive Boulevard, Elmsford, New York 10523, 1-(800) 669-7464
Website: www. minusone.com • E-mail: mmomus@aol.com